ZELL & LURIE

"Sam Zell and Robert H. Lurie Partnership Impact on American Real Estate"

TUNDEX RR. ROTIO

TABLE OF CONTENTS

CHAPTER 1

THE FOUNDING PARTNERSHIP

1.1 The Meeting of Minds: Zell and Lurie's Early Connection

The partnership between Sam Zell and Robert H. Lurie is a tale of remarkable synergy, as two exceptional minds united to create a real estate journey that few could rival.

The origins of this strong partnership can be traced to the University of Michigan, where Zell and Lurie first met in the early 1960s.

Zell, a Chicago-born individual with bold self-assurance, was working towards his law degree. Lurie recognized for his careful intellect and reserved personality, was additionally attracted to business and investment.

Despite their differing personalities, both individuals possessed a strong entrepreneurial spirit, a sharp perception of opportunity, and a readiness to embrace calculated risks—traits that would shape their success in the future.

Their initial connection developed through common interests. Zell, a natural hustler, gained recognition for his initial ventures in the realm of real estate.

While still a student, he oversaw rental properties, utilizing his keen ability to identify opportunities and negotiate agreements. Lurie, just as ambitious but more analytical, was captivated by Zell's method. Their bond wasn't immediate, yet they soon identified in one another a matching skill set that, when merged, could become a formidable power.

While Zell contributed a dynamic, rapid energy, Lurie's reflective strategy offered equilibrium. This dynamic would serve as a foundation of their partnership.

Initially, their relationship was primarily social, since they were part of the same circles at the University of Michigan.

However, the two quickly discovered that they could gain knowledge from each other, with each providing perspectives that the other may not have thought of. Zell's rapid decision-making and limitless enthusiasm motivated Lurie to adopt a more entrepreneurial mindset. On the other hand, Zell valued Lurie's careful and strategic method regarding finance and investments.

Their bond grew stronger through numerous conversations regarding market trends, investment prospects, and business ideologies. It didn't take long for them to start imagining what they could accomplish together.

The concept of collaborating was driven by their mutual restlessness. Zell and Lurie were motivated by the opportunity to create something impactful during a period when the American real estate market was ready for change.

In the economic boom after the war, real estate was transforming, leading to new investment prospects nationwide.

Zell and Lurie recognized the industry's potential, particularly in undervalued assets, and believed that their distinct mix of audacity and prudence could enable them to seize these opportunities in ways others might miss.

This shared acknowledgment of potential would lay the groundwork for their iconic collaboration.

1.2 Building the Foundation: Shared Values and Vision

In establishing their partnership, Zell and Lurie shared a core philosophy that would guide their collaborative efforts: the quest for value and the conviction that success arises from taking smart risks. For Zell, the concept of risk was thrilling.

He was recognized for his readiness to engage in high-risk projects, frequently wagering on undervalued real estate and troubled assets that few others would contemplate.

Lurie, in contrast, tackled risk with a strategic mindset, consistently evaluating the long-term consequences of every choice.

They collaboratively created a balanced strategy, with Zell's boldness moderated by Lurie's prudence, forming a synergy that enabled them to optimize returns while maintaining stability. The duo exhibited a strong work ethic and dedication to achieving excellence.

Zell and Lurie were recognized for their practical approach, frequently engaging deeply in the specifics of each deal.

They held the conviction of grasping each aspect of a contract before proceeding, a guideline that assisted them in steering clear of typical errors. This commitment to thoroughness became a hallmark of their collaboration.

In contrast to numerous investors who merely observed from a distance, Zell and Lurie were deeply involved with the properties they acquired, comprehending the markets, neighborhoods, and local elements that could affect value. This method enabled them to make better-informed choices and resulted in steady success.

A core principle that Zell and Lurie embraced was to consistently "do the opposite." This opposing philosophy emerged as a pivotal influence in their commercial transactions.

Where others perceived downturn, Zell and Lurie frequently recognized potential. This viewpoint was particularly clear in their funding of troubled properties, an area frequently ignored or disregarded by conventional investors.

To Zell and Lurie, though, these assets possessed unexploited potential. Through the acquisition and revitalization of these properties, they generated substantial value and simultaneously supported the economic growth of the communities in which they invested.

Their common vision went beyond merely generating profits. Zell and Lurie were dedicated to creating a lasting legacy, an empire that would withstand economic fluctuations and keep expanding with time.

They were tactical in their purchases, frequently targeting properties that could increase in value over the long haul.

This long-term outlook distinguished them from other investors who mainly concentrated on immediate profits. Zell and Lurie recognized that genuine wealth developed over decades rather than just years, and this realization influenced every choice they made.

One of the most crucial elements of their collaboration was the respect and trust they had for each other. Zell and Lurie shared a silent agreement, an inherent trust that enabled them to decide quickly and efficiently.

In the realm of high-stakes real estate, where fortunes could vanish in an instant, this trust was indispensable.

They frequently required neither extensive talks nor official contracts; a handshake and a common goal sufficed to progress. This degree of trust, uncommon in business, was established over years of collaboration and became a characteristic aspect of their relationship. A crucial element of their common vision was their dedication to innovation.

Zell and Lurie were dissatisfied with adhering to industry standards; they aimed to transform them. This push for innovation prompted them to explore new business models and strategies that had not been attempted previously.

For instance, Zell's initial contributions to real estate investment trusts (REITs) played a significant role in transforming the real estate sector, offering investors a novel way to engage with property markets.

Lurie's financial expertise played a crucial role in the success of these ventures, as he structured deals to reduce risk and enhance returns. United, they developed a framework for achievement that would be replicated by upcoming generations of investors.

Central to their collaboration was a profound sense of purpose. Zell and Lurie weren't solely focused on profit; they were motivated by a passion to build something significant.

They aimed to create a legacy, establishing a company that would endure over time and contribute positively to the industry. This sense of purpose filled their work with a mission, motivating those nearby to pursue excellence. Workers, associates, and customers all experienced the enthusiasm and dedication that Zell and Lurie infused into their tasks, and this fervor turned into a key factor in their achievements.

In the subsequent years, Zell and Lurie would develop a real estate empire that transformed the American landscape.

Their collaboration, rooted in common values and an ambitious vision, allowed them to attain remarkable success in a fiercely competitive sector.

United, they faced challenges, forged new paths, and made a lasting impact on the realm of real estate. Their narrative serves as proof of the strength of collaboration, illustrating how two people with varying abilities and viewpoints can unite to accomplish remarkable things.

CHAPTER 2

TRANSFORMING THE REAL ESTATE INDUSTRY

2.1 Breaking New Ground: Early Ventures and Acquisitions

Sam Zell and Robert H. Lurie began their transformation of the American real estate industry through a series of early investments and acquisitions that would position them as trailblazers in the sector.

These initial years were characterized by a steep learning trajectory, an unyielding quest for worth, and a sharp awareness of overlooked prospects.

By experimenting and balancing their distinct blend of boldness and prudence,

Zell and Lurie built a base that would allow them to expand and enhance their impact throughout the country.

Their early ventures in real estate were not part of a major, strategic scheme, but instead the outcome of taking advantage of opportunities when they arose.

Zell, recognized for his charming and bold personality, started purchasing properties while he was still a law student at the University of Michigan.

His initial transactions were minor—primarily student rentals and affordable residential properties—but these experiences educated him on the basics of property management and acquisition.

Zell promptly identified the opportunity to produce substantial cash flow from real estate, particularly in properties that others could disregard.

His initial achievements formed a blueprint for subsequent transactions, enabling him to enhance his grasp of asset valuation, tenant interactions, and the strength of utilizing undervalued assets.

During these early years, Zell's collaboration with Lurie was extremely beneficial. Lurie's analytical and cautious style complemented Zell's ambitious drive, forming a dynamic that was uncommon in the real estate industry.

When Zell spotted a property with low value, Lurie would carefully examine the financial records, evaluate possible risks, and devise strategies to enhance the asset's worth. This collaborative method enabled them to forge new paths while reducing unnecessary risk, establishing a mutually beneficial situation that would define their identity.

One of their initial victories stemmed from investing in troubled properties, an idea that was fairly unexplored in the conventional real estate market then.

The U.S. economy during the 1970s was unstable, facing inflationary pressures and energy crises that impacted industries across the country.

For Zell and Lurie, this upheaval, however, offered a chance. Where others perceived danger, they recognized the possibility of great gain. By purchasing undervalued distressed assets, they had the opportunity to restore these properties, stabilize them, and ultimately sell them for substantial profits.

This method of distressed investing became a hallmark strategy, leading them to purchase multiple properties and transform struggling assets into successful enterprises.

A significant purchase that established their initial reputation was a collection of office buildings in Chicago.

At that moment, office spaces were experiencing elevated vacancy levels and low tenant retention, resulting in a sense of uncertainty. Zell and Lurie, nevertheless, understood that these obstacles were not permanent. They recognized the worth of Chicago's property market and had faith in its potential for long-term expansion.

By securing beneficial purchase conditions, they obtained the buildings at a significant reduction.

Their tactical enhancements and assertive leasing initiatives quickly transformed these properties into lucrative assets, showcasing their capacity to recognize and exploit market inefficiencies.

Their achievement with office properties prompted an expansion into additional sectors, such as multifamily housing and retail areas. Zell and Lurie understood that diversifying would be essential for minimizing risk and enhancing growth.

They put their money into apartment complexes, shopping malls, and even industrial properties, using the same strategies that had benefited them with office spaces.

This diversification of their portfolio enabled them to distribute risk across various sectors, ensuring that a decline in one sector wouldn't significantly affect their total assets.

Zell and Lurie's knack for identifying trends and adjusting to market needs became fundamental to their approach, distinguishing them from conventional real estate investors who usually concentrated on one asset class.

2.2 Innovation and Risk: Redefining Real Estate Norms

What genuinely distinguished Zell and Lurie was their readiness to innovate in a famously conservative industry.

They understood that the real estate market was ready for upheaval, and they were willing to challenge limits to reach their objectives.

One of the most significant innovations was Zell's groundbreaking contributions to real estate investment trusts (REITs), a framework that would ultimately revolutionize the real estate sector.

REITs enabled ordinary investors to possess stakes in real estate properties, democratizing entry to a market that was typically exclusive to wealthy individuals and institutional investors.

Zell recognized that REITs could not only gather funds but also open up a fresh path for expansion in the real estate industry.

During the 1980s, Zell started promoting publicly-traded REITs as a means to grow his real estate investments.

He viewed REITs as a means to offer liquidity, capital access, and tax benefits for investors, enabling them to engage in the real estate market without requiring substantial personal funds.

By classifying his assets as publicly traded companies, Zell successfully raised billions of dollars, which he then utilized to purchase additional properties and further diversify his investments.

This groundbreaking method not only aided Zell and Lurie's enterprise but also transformed the perception of real estate investment, drawing a fresh influx of investors into the sector.

The achievement of Zell's REIT model created pathways to larger prospects.

He persisted in forming intricate agreements that utilized the tax advantages and liquidity of REITs, enabling him to pursue acquisitions that would have been unachievable with conventional funding methods. Zell's REITs emerged as some of the largest in the nation, featuring a diverse range of assets, such as office buildings, residential units, and retail centers.

The achievements of these REITs showcased Zell and Lurie's capacity to move past traditional approaches and reshape industry standards, reinforcing their standing as innovative trailblazers.

Accompanying this growth was a heightened openness to take risks in ways that few within the industry would contemplate.

For Zell and Lurie, risk wasn't an aspect to evade but rather a resource to be strategically handled. They understood that effective investing necessitated daring actions, but they were also acutely conscious of the possible repercussions of errors.

Their method for managing risk entailed thorough research, scenario analysis, and a steadfast dedication to due diligence.

Zell and Lurie would devote hours to examining market trends, economic information, and political elements that might influence their investments.

By grasping the complete range of risks tied to each transaction, they could make knowledgeable choices that weighed potential benefits against likely drawbacks.

One of their boldest actions was their foray into global markets, a territory that few U.S. real estate investors had explored.

Zell and Lurie recognized the opportunities for expansion in emerging markets and started investing in real estate beyond the United States.

This decision necessitated a thorough comprehension of international markets, local laws, and cultural subtleties.

Zell and Lurie tackled these global endeavors with the same mix of audacity and prudence that characterized their achievements at home.

Through comprehensive research and collaboration with local specialists, they successfully maneuvered through these intricate markets, once again establishing a new benchmark for the sector. Another domain where Zell and Lurie transformed standards was their emphasis on troubled debt.

In times of economic decline, they frequently bought debt from distressed firms at discounted rates, a tactic enabling them to obtain valuable assets for less than market value.

This method demanded a profound comprehension of the financial environment and a readiness to manage the complexities of debt restructuring.

Zell and Lurie's knowledge of distressed debt allowed them to obtain assets that many considered overly risky, transforming these investments into lucrative opportunities.

Their achievements in this field further bolstered their image as astute investors capable of transforming risk into opportunity.

Zell and Lurie's readiness to adopt innovation went further than just financial frameworks and investment methods.

They were recognized for their innovative methods in property management and tenant interactions.

Zell, in particular, thought that a practical approach was crucial for optimizing the worth of their assets. He would personally check properties, talk to tenants, and pinpoint areas that need enhancement. This degree of engagement was uncommon for a real estate tycoon of Zell's caliber, yet it showcased his dedication to upholding quality standards and guaranteeing tenant contentment.

Zell and Lurie's focus on customer service set a standard for the industry, underscoring the significance of regarding tenants as collaborators instead of just sources of income.

A significant legacy of Zell and Lurie's method was how they motivated a new cohort of real estate experts to embrace innovative thinking. Their readiness to question conventional standards, adopt new ideas, and undertake thoughtful risks established a new benchmark for the sector. Zell and Lurie showed that real estate could be tackled with the same innovation and adaptability as other sectors, paving the way for upcoming investors to investigate fresh concepts and expand the limits of possibility.

By reshaping real estate standards, Zell and Lurie created a thriving company and simultaneously revolutionized the industry.

Their influence is evident in the broad acceptance of REITs, the increasing interest in distressed debt investing, and the focus on customer service in real estate management.

They demonstrated that real estate involves more than just structures and property; it's about generating value, supporting communities, and making a meaningful difference.

The path of Zell and Lurie from modest investors to industry legends showcases the strength of creativity and boldness in business.

Their initial ventures and acquisitions established a foundation for a novel strategy in real estate, whereas their openness to innovation transformed the realm of possibilities.

By pioneering innovative approaches and questioning established norms, Zell and Lurie revolutionized the American real estate sector, creating a legacy that still motivates and impacts today.

CHAPTER 3

THE EXPANSION YEARS

3.1 Entering New Markets: Diversification and Growth Strategies

By the early 1980s, Sam Zell and Robert H. Lurie had attained significant success in the real estate sector, yet their aspirations were still unfulfilled.

The pair understood that to attain sustainable, lasting growth, they must go beyond conventional real estate investments and venture into new markets.

This belief resulted in a significant phase in their collaboration, marked by bold diversification and the creation of a very strategic method for growth. They were no longer merely real estate investors—they were innovating a new business model that merged the boundaries of real estate, finance, and corporate investment.

A primary growth strategy that Zell and Lurie implemented was to spread their investments across different asset classes and regions.

Initially concentrating on office buildings and apartment complexes in Chicago, they quickly recognized that restricting their investments to a single city or sector subjected them to avoidable risks.

By diversifying into various markets, they could take advantage of growth prospects in one region while another region might lag. This approach would not only assist them in creating a more robust portfolio but also enable them to endure the unavoidable fluctuations of economic cycles.

Their initial move towards diversification included venturing into the retail and industrial property markets.

Retail properties, including shopping centers and malls, presented significant cash flow opportunities, whereas industrial sites, like warehouses and manufacturing plants, ensured consistent income through long-term leases.

Zell and Lurie acknowledged that every sector possessed distinct traits and necessitated varied management strategies. They created dedicated teams for every asset category, guaranteeing that their properties were overseen by specialists who grasped the subtleties of each market.

This commitment to specialization became a defining feature of their operations, enabling them to optimize returns across various investments.

Their move into industrial properties turned out to be particularly wise as the logistics sector started to thrive in the 1980s.

As global trade expands and supply chain efficiency becomes more critical, the need for warehouse and distribution centers has grown significantly.

Zell and Lurie were among the pioneers to identify this trend, purchasing industrial real estate in key areas close to significant transportation centers.

Their skill in recognizing and taking advantage of new market trends provided them with a competitive advantage, enabling them to secure advantageous lease agreements and create a solid footing in the industrial sector ahead of other investors.

Along with diversifying among asset classes, Zell and Lurie also broadened their geographical reach. Acknowledging the drawbacks of concentrating only on Chicago, they started to obtain properties in other significant urban centers throughout the United States. Cities such as Los Angeles, New York, and Miami presented unique opportunities and challenges, prompting Zell and Lurie to customize their strategies for each market.

For instance, in Los Angeles, they concentrated on real estate that served the entertainment and technology sectors, whereas in New York, they put their money into sought-after office locations in Manhattan.

This expansion into various markets enabled them to diversify their risk and take advantage. One of their most significant endeavors beyond Chicago was the purchase of several properties in the Sun Belt, a region that is seeing fast population growth attributed to pleasant weather, reduced living expenses, and pro-business regulations.

Zell and Lurie understood that the growing appeal of the Sun Belt would result in higher demand for both residential and commercial properties, positioning it as a perfect region for expansion.

They started purchasing apartment complexes, office spaces, and retail centers in cities such as Phoenix, Dallas, and Atlanta.

This action turned out to be very successful, as the area kept expanding, drawing in both companies and inhabitants. By venturing into these developing markets early, Zell and Lurie managed to create a strong presence and gain from the economic surge in the area.

Zell and Lurie's strategy for diversification extended beyond just real estate. In a daring decision, they started seeking opportunities beyond conventional real estate investments, such as investing in troubled assets and corporate acquisitions.

By purchasing shares in failing businesses, they could utilize their turnaround skills and real estate insights to reveal concealed worth.

This approach signified the start of their shift from real estate investors to varied corporate financiers. One of their initial achievements in this field was obtaining a controlling interest in a manufacturing firm that was close to insolvency.

Zell and Lurie reorganized the business, reset its debt agreements, and divested non-essential assets, ultimately transforming it into a successful company.

Their foray into corporate buyouts turned out to be one of their most lucrative diversification strategies, resulting in their acquisition of stakes in businesses spanning several sectors, such as manufacturing, energy, and finance.

These corporate investments not only yielded substantial returns but also established them as powerful participants in the wider business landscape. Zell and

Lurie were no longer regarded solely as real estate tycoons but as insightful investors possessing a sharp grasp of business strategy and corporate governance.

This varied strategy allowed them to lessen dependence on a specific asset class, resulting in a strong and durable portfolio capable of enduring market changes.

3.2 Adjusting to Economic Changes: Managing Property Market Cycles

The real estate sector is naturally cyclical, characterized by phases of fast expansion frequently succeeded by declines. Zell and Lurie recognized that to endure and succeed in this landscape, they had to excel at adjusting to economic changes.

Their skill in predicting and reacting to economic shifts emerged as one of their key advantages, enabling them to not just endure recessions but to transform them into chances for expansion.

A significant early economic hurdle they encountered was the recession of the early 1980s, characterized by elevated inflation, increasing interest rates, and stagnant growth.

Numerous real estate investors faced challenges during this time, as borrowing expenses increased and property prices fell. Zell and Lurie, nonetheless, were ready. They had taken a cautious strategy regarding leverage, making sure they did not overreach with too much debt. This caution enabled them to preserve liquidity and evade the financial pressure that affected numerous rivals.

Zell and Lurie's expertise with troubled assets was extremely helpful during times of economic decline. As property values fell, they recognized chances to obtain premium assets for a small portion of their former worth.

In the recession of the 1980s, they started acquiring troubled properties from banks and financial institutions that were keen to sell off non-performing assets.

By purchasing these properties at reduced prices, Zell and Lurie managed to create a significant portfolio of assets that would increase in value as the economy improved. Their readiness to invest in uncertain times distinguished them from other investors who were immobilized by fear.

The cyclical characteristics of real estate likewise educated Zell and Lurie on the significance of adaptability in their business strategy.

They realized that varying economic conditions necessitated distinct investment approaches.

In times of economic expansion, they concentrated on lucrative investments, like office properties and retail spaces, that prospered in a flourishing economy.

Nevertheless, in times of downturns, they redirected their attention to more secure assets, like apartment buildings and industrial real estate, which ensured consistent cash flow even during difficult periods.

This flexible strategy enabled them to navigate economic changes and keep producing revenue no matter the market situation.

Zell and Lurie's knack for adaptation was showcased again during the savings and loan crisis of the late 1980s and early 1990s, a time characterized by the failure of countless savings and loan institutions throughout the United States.

The crisis resulted in a surge of foreclosures and troubled properties, establishing a buyer's market for investors who had capital to invest. Zell and Lurie viewed this as a prime chance.

They started acquiring foreclosed properties from the Resolution Trust Corporation (RTC), a governmental entity responsible for overseeing the assets of failed savings and loans.

This approach enabled them to obtain properties at greatly lowered costs, setting them up to gain when the market rebounded.

Their flexibility went beyond acquiring assets to include financing strategies as well. Zell and Lurie were trailblazers in utilizing Real Estate Investment Trusts (REITs) for capital generation. By marketing their assets as publicly-traded REITs, they gained access to public markets for financing, giving them a reliable source of capital that was less reliant on conventional debt.

This development enabled them to retain financial flexibility and lessen their dependence on bank loans, which were frequently hard to obtain during economic recessions.

Incorporating REITs emerged as a key element of their financial approach, offering the liquidity essential for ongoing expansion despite tough economic conditions.

Besides economic cycles, Zell and Lurie also had to manage shifts in government policy and regulation, which significantly influenced the real estate sector. They watched regulatory changes carefully and modified their strategies as needed.

For instance, when tax regulations were altered to restrict the advantages of depreciation for real estate investors, Zell and Lurie redirected their attention to areas where the updated rules had minimal effect.

Their capacity to adjust to regulatory shifts enabled them to stay competitive and steer clear of the traps that surprised many of their counterparts.

During their growth years, Zell and Lurie showcased an impressive capability to adjust to shifting economic circumstances.

Their strategic method for diversification and their readiness to adopt novel financial frameworks allowed them to maneuver through economic cycles and come out more resilient after each downturn.

By merging a long-term perspective with an adaptable investment strategy, Zell and Lurie created a company capable of enduring the natural fluctuations of the real estate sector.

Their achievements throughout these growth years established the groundwork for a business empire that would persist in expanding and transforming, making a significant mark on the American real estate sector.

In summary, the years of expansion marked a time of significant growth and change for Sam Zell and Robert H. Lurie.

Using strategic diversification, they ventured into new markets and established a strong portfolio that covered various asset classes and areas.

Their capacity to maneuver through economic fluctuations and adjust to evolving market scenarios showcased their resilience and vision, traits that would characterize their legacy as two of the most impactful personalities in contemporary real estate.

CHAPTER 4

REVOLUTIONIZING COMMERCIAL REAL ESTATE

4.1 The Creation of REITs: A New Model for Investment

The transformation that Sam Zell and Robert H. Lurie introduced to the real estate sector extended past merely buying and overseeing properties; they aimed to fundamentally change the way individuals invested in real estate.

One of their most significant contributions was their groundbreaking development of Real Estate Investment Trusts, or REITs, a framework that provided ordinary investors with opportunities in commercial real estate. Zell, frequently referred to as the "Grave Dancer" due to his opposing investment strategies, gained recognition as the "Father of the Modern REIT" for his efforts in transforming this idea into a robust investment tool.

By utilizing REITs, Zell and Lurie made commercial real estate investing accessible to a broader audience, which had formerly been restricted to institutional investors and affluent individuals.

The idea of a REIT wasn't unfamiliar in the 1980s, but the framework had not yet gained widespread success or acknowledgment. In the 1960s, Congress established the REIT model to enable individuals to invest in extensive, income-generating real estate, much like investing in stocks. Nevertheless, REITs encountered constraints in their initial years, mainly because of strict tax and operational regulations.

Zell and Lurie identified a chance to transform REITs into a compelling and viable investment by enhancing their efficiency, flexibility, and ability to produce stable returns.

Their participation was instrumental in establishing REITs as a fundamental element of the real estate sector. Zell's foray into the REIT market commenced with his oversight of underperforming REITs that had suffered due to inadequate management and economic pressure. His approach centered on obtaining underachieving REITs, reorganizing them, and introducing expert management.

Zell was convinced that effectively managed REITs could reveal substantial value, so he focused heavily on minimizing overhead, eliminating unnecessary expenses, and adopting tactics to enhance rental income and asset worth.

He turned REITs from inactive holding firms into vibrant enterprises with engaged management teams focused on enhancing returns.

In the early 1990s, Zell made a significant impact in the REIT sector by founding Equity Residential, which specialized in owning and overseeing apartment complexes.

He capitalized on the decline in real estate by acquiring troubled assets at bargain prices, and by incorporating them into a REIT, he enabled individual investors to gain from these investments.

Equity Residential evolved into a very prosperous REIT, offering consistent earnings to investors while achieving significant increases in capital value.

Zell's achievements with Equity Residential showcased the capabilities of REITs as an impactful investment strategy and garnered significant interest. Zell's involvement with REITs extended beyond Equity Residential.

He went on to create a range of REITs that focused on various property types, such as office buildings, industrial sites, and retail spaces.

Every REIT was customized to the unique traits of its asset class, featuring a management approach aimed at optimizing returns within that sector.

For instance, Equity Office Properties concentrated on premium office structures in key areas, whereas Equity Industrial Partners aimed at warehouses and logistics facilities.

By broadening his REIT portfolio, Zell was able to provide investors with various choices tailored to distinct risk levels and income objectives. A defining feature of Zell's REITs was their capacity to utilize economies of scale.

By consolidating a vast array of properties into one entity, Zell was able to secure improved conditions with suppliers, obtain lower-cost financing, and deploy cost-saving technologies throughout his collection.

This strategy enabled his REITs to function more effectively than smaller, privately owned real estate companies, resulting in greater returns for investors.

Additionally, since REITs must distribute a significant portion of their taxable income to shareholders, Zell's REITs provided appealing dividend yields, which made them desirable for investors focused on income.

The establishment of REITs marked a significant milestone in the real estate sector, transforming how individuals invested in property.

Before REITs, commercial real estate was primarily the territory of affluent investors and institutional entities.

Through the creation of REITs as a feasible investment option, Zell and Lurie enabled individual investors to possess a stake in prime real estate in key cities throughout the United States. This democratization of real estate investment broadened the investor base, enhanced market liquidity, and ultimately aided in the growth and stability of the real estate sector.

REITs also introduced increased transparency to the real estate market. As publicly listed companies, Zell's REITs were under regulatory supervision and had to reveal financial details to their investors.

This clarity enabled investors to make educated choices and enhanced the trustworthiness of REITs as a type of investment. Over the years, REITs evolved into a favored option for retirement portfolios and various long-term investment strategies, providing a blend of income and growth opportunities.

Zell significantly influenced the REIT sector, and his achievements motivated other real estate investors to emulate his path.

By the end of the 1990s, the REIT industry had expanded considerably, featuring many REITs on prominent stock exchanges and encompassing a diverse range of property categories.

Zell's perspective on REITs contributed to a stronger, more accessible, and lucrative real estate market, and his impact on the industry is still evident today.

4.2 Iconic Transactions: Significant Properties and Remarkable Deals

Though Zell and Lurie were recognized for their tactical method in real estate, several of their transactions stood out not only for their monetary achievements but also for their influence on the industry and the prestigious nature of the properties in question.

Their collection featured some of the most iconic and valuable properties in the United States, and their skill in spotting, purchasing, and improving these assets established their status as leaders in the commercial real estate industry.

One of Zell's most notable deals was his purchase of the Chicago-based Equity Office Properties Trust in the late 1990s.

At that time, this REIT was the biggest owner of office properties in the United States, holding a portfolio comprising key office buildings in major cities such as New York, San Francisco, and Washington, D.C.

The purchase of Equity Office Properties was a daring decision that highlighted Zell's belief in the enduring worth of office real estate.

The agreement represented a huge effort, encompassing billions of dollars and intricate financing deals, yet Zell's knowledge and standing drew in the required funds to realize it. The Equity Office Properties deal was significant not just for its size but also for the creative strategy Zell employed in overseeing the portfolio.

He presented a concept of "active management," which entailed meticulously overseeing the performance of each building and making alterations to optimize occupancy and rental revenue.

By prioritizing operational efficiency and tenant contentment, Zell managed to enhance the portfolio's value, turning Equity Office Properties into one of the most lucrative REITs in the industry.

Another significant agreement was Zell's participation in the purchase of the property portfolio from the distressed Resolution Trust Corporation (RTC) following the savings and loan crisis.

The RTC was a governmental body tasked with dissolving assets from unsuccessful savings and loan institutions, and its inventory encompassed a large number of troubled properties nationwide.

Zell and Lurie recognized a chance to purchase these assets at greatly reduced prices, enabling them to create a substantial and varied portfolio of properties with considerable growth potential.

The RTC acquisition demonstrated Zell and Lurie's capacity to leverage market disruptions and their readiness to embrace risks for the sake of long-term benefits.

By purchasing distressed properties at bargain prices, they could achieve significant profits as the real estate market bounced back.

This deal highlighted Zell and Lurie's status as contrarian investors capable of identifying value in places where others perceived only danger.

Their achievements with the RTC portfolio strengthened their role as innovators in the real estate sector and cemented their impact on commercial real estate investments.

Zell's skill in identifying the potential of underpriced properties also prompted him to invest in renowned hotels and resorts.

One of his most significant purchases was the iconic Blackstone Hotel in Chicago, a historic establishment that had deteriorated over time.

Zell recognized the opportunity to rejuvenate the hotel to its original splendor and turn it into a lucrative investment. He put money into renovations, modernized the amenities, and rebranded the hotel as a top choice for business guests and tourists.

The achievement of the Blackstone Hotel initiative showcased Zell's dedication to maintaining and improving landmark properties, contributing another facet to his legacy as a real estate investor. Throughout their careers, Zell and Lurie's deals were motivated by a dedication to enhancing value, whether via strategic acquisitions, operational enhancements, or creative management approaches.

Their emphasis on generating long-term value for their investors distinguished them from other real estate investors who favored immediate profits.

This approach enabled them to develop a collection of iconic properties that not only produced significant returns but also added to the architectural and cultural fabric of American cities.

Zell and Lurie's method for real estate transactions was marked by careful preparation, courageous choices, and a readiness to defy conventions.

They were unafraid to engage in intricate, high-risk transactions if they had faith in the long-term prospects of the assets concerned.

Their legendary agreements turned into case studies within the industry, highlighting the significance of vision, patience, and flexibility in attaining success in commercial real estate.

To summarize, the establishment of REITs and the pivotal deals by Zell and Lurie were essential in transforming the real estate sector. Their initiatives to promote REITs made commercial real estate available to a wider audience, while their renowned transactions established new benchmarks for quality and creativity in property management.

Collectively, these accomplishments positioned Zell and Lurie as pivotal figures whose impact on the real estate sector is still evident today.

CHAPTER 5

THE ART OF DEAL-MAKING

5.1 Negotiation Tactics: The Zell & Lurie Approach

In the realm of real estate, where triumph frequently depends on obtaining advantageous agreements, few excelled in the craft of negotiation quite like Sam Zell and Robert H. Lurie.

Renowned for their keen intuition, inventive negotiation techniques, and profound insight into human behavior, Zell and Lurie crafted a strategy that allowed them to transform tough negotiations into successful agreements.

Their approach was characterized by a mix of patience, confidence, and the skill to craft an engaging story around every transaction, rendering their collaboration powerful in boardrooms and negotiation tables nationwide.

Central to Zell and Lurie's negotiation strategies was their dedication to thorough preparation. Zell is well-known for asserting that in every negotiation, "information is strength."

Before finalizing a deal, he and Lurie would perform extensive research, scrutinizing all aspects of the property, the market conditions, and the seller's motivations.

They recognized that each party arrived with distinct pressures, priorities, and limitations, and by grasping these dynamics, they could strategize to exploit weaknesses or identify shared interests.

Zell was recognized for his skill in discerning the other party's intentions, frequently predicting their actions, and responding with strategies that utilized his informational edge effectively.

Preparation, though, was merely the basis of their strategy. Zell and Lurie excelled at tailoring their negotiation approaches to the unique situations of every agreement.

If they detected uncertainty or fear from the opposing side, they could take on a more calming, supportive tone, fostering connection and alleviating the perceived risk for the seller. When urgency was a concern, Zell was unafraid to take a more forceful stance, advocating for quick decisions to seize time-sensitive chances.

Their skill in switching roles, transitioning from amicable partner to tough rival, enabled them to repeatedly stay in front.

A notable strategy of Zell's was his readiness to back out of a deal. He perceived negotiations as a reciprocal process where both parties had to seek value, and if he believed that an agreement did not align with his expectations or his vision for success, he was not hesitant to walk away.

This strategy wasn't merely a deception; Zell maintained high standards for himself and his team and only sought deals that offered evident value.

This approach of selective commitment also provided him with an advantage, since he wasn't perceived as desperate or too eager.

Sellers and investors understood that if Zell expressed interest, the agreement was probably favorable, and if he opted out, it signified that the proposal was insufficient.

This assurance in stepping away turned into a formidable negotiation asset, enabling Zell to influence discussions according to his conditions.

Additionally, Zell and Lurie excelled in crafting a story for every transaction. They understood that real estate transactions involve more than just figures; they are frequently shaped by feelings, perceptions, and aspirations for the future.

By articulating their vision effectively, Zell and Lurie frequently managed to influence sellers and investors who were initially reluctant.

They would describe how the property aligned with their overall strategy, their plans to increase its value, and the mutual benefits of finalizing the agreement.

This story development proved especially successful with troubled assets, as Zell was able to highlight his history of revitalizing properties, reassuring sellers that they were entrusting their assets to skilled hands.

Zell and Lurie recognized the significance of timing as well. In numerous instances, they would tactically postpone or hasten discussions according to market circumstances, seasonal demand, or the financial status of the sellers.

They frequently purchased properties in economic downturns when prices dropped, and they would strategically plan their exits to align with high-demand peaks.

This timing approach demanded both patience and vision, as Zell and Lurie occasionally spent years before seeing their profits. Their skill in forecasting market trends and adapting their negotiations accordingly enabled them to regularly purchase at low prices and sell at high ones.

Another unique feature of Zell's negotiation approach was his frank, direct manner of communication.

He had minimal tolerance for embellishments or ulterior motives and liked to tackle problems head-on, occasionally with a degree of straightforwardness that surprised those around him.

This openness, while sometimes harsh, frequently earned him respect and confidence. He thought that openness and truthfulness cultivated trust, simplifying the establishment of lasting connections with sellers, investors, and partners.

Individuals understood their position with Zell, and his standing for integrity provided him an advantage in negotiations.

In the end, the negotiation method of Zell and Lurie was founded on discipline and determination. They never let feelings interfere with their decision-making, and they consistently kept a sharp focus on their ultimate goals.

Each transaction was viewed as a component of a broader strategy, not merely an isolated deal. This comprehensive perspective empowered them to make choices that aligned with their broader objectives, even if it required sacrificing immediate profits for future benefits.

Zell and Lurie's methodical negotiation techniques, along with their flexibility and strategic thinking, distinguished them from rivals and reinforced their status as expert dealmakers.

5.2 Balancing Act: High-Risk Investments and Cautionary Moves

Sam Zell and Robert Lurie were naturally inclined to take risks, yet they were never careless. Their method of handling risk was measured, thoughtful, and based on a thorough comprehension of market trends and financial caution. They maintained that significant returns frequently demanded courageous decisions, yet they recognized the necessity of risk management to prevent devastating losses.

This careful balancing of high-risk investments with cautious strategies became a hallmark of their partnership and a key factor in their continued success.

One of the main strategies used by Zell and Lurie to manage risk involved the careful selection of assets that had inherent value, regardless of whether they were presently underperforming or in distress.

They frequently focused on properties that were overlooked or undervalued because of mismanagement, economic pressure, or adverse market situations.

By concentrating on assets with fundamental potential, they might lower the risks tied to their investments.

For instance, instead of guessing about expensive properties in flourishing markets, they frequently purchased troubled assets for a small percentage of their actual worth.

This strategy enabled them to achieve significant returns while reducing downside risk, as they could either sell the asset or enhance its performance to regain their original investment.

Zell's famous "Grave Dancer" tactic exemplified this method. He thought that, similar to a "vulture capitalist," he could restore failing assets by purchasing them at low costs, reorganizing operations, and rejuvenating them.

This approach carried inherent risks since troubled assets present considerable difficulties, yet Zell and Lurie reduced these risks by performing thorough due diligence.

They meticulously evaluated the possibility for transformation, closely examining elements such as site, management track record, and market needs.

By strategically investing in overlooked assets, they transformed properties that others neglected into lucrative opportunities.

Alongside their emphasis on undervalued assets, Zell and Lurie were careful with their financial structuring.

They frequently used leverage to enhance their returns, yet they did it in a manner that reduced their vulnerability to market fluctuations.

For instance, Zell often utilized non-recourse loans, enabling him to obtain financing without personally backing the obligation. This arrangement ensured that if a project did not succeed, his personal belongings were not in jeopardy.

Zell and Lurie were also recognized for their commitment to keeping cash reserves, enabling them to endure economic slumps without having to conduct fire sales.

This financial caution proved especially beneficial during downturns, allowing them to purchase distressed properties while others were liquidating at a loss.

Zell and Lurie's risky investments were frequently offset by prudent actions that ensured stability.

A key strategy they employed was diversification. By creating a portfolio that encompassed various property types— like office complexes, residential units, shopping centers, and manufacturing sites—they could balance losses in one area with profits in another. This variety assisted them in handling the inherent risks associated with the real estate market, which can be influenced by economic cycles, interest rates, and shifts in consumer behavior.

Zell and Lurie's capacity to spread their investments over various asset classes and geographical areas enabled them to sustain consistent growth, even when particular sectors encountered difficulties.

Another important element of their risk management approach was Zell's emphasis on timing. He gained recognition for his opposing investment approach, frequently purchasing when others were offloading and the other way around. This method demanded not just courage but also a sharp awareness of market timing.

Zell and Lurie would invest in markets during periods of decline when prices dropped, retaining assets until the market situation got better.

They were long-term investors who avoided seeking fast profits, and their skill in aligning their investments with market trends reduced their vulnerability to speculative risks.

This approach also enabled them to capitalize on chances that others overlooked, as they frequently were the only purchasers in a struggling market.

A prominent illustration of Zell's astute timing and risk management was his divestiture of Equity Office Properties in 2007, right before the global financial crisis.

Zell sold the office REIT to Blackstone for $39 billion, marking the largest leveraged buyout in history at that moment.

This transaction was viewed as a brilliant stroke of timing since the property market fell apart just after.

By selling at the height, Zell ensured a substantial profit for his investors and steered clear of the devastating losses that affected the market in the years that followed.

This action demonstrated Zell's ability to evaluate market trends and take decisive steps to safeguard his investments.

Even with their daring actions, Zell and Lurie consistently anticipated worst-case situations. They acknowledged that the real estate market might be erratic and uncertain, and they prepared accordingly.

Their agreements were designed to incorporate exit strategies, backup plans, and financial safeguards that shielded them from potential losses.

This careful method of organizing agreements guaranteed that, despite challenges, they could maintain their funds and bounce back from setbacks. Their systematic method of managing risk played a crucial role in their durability and achievement in an industry recognized for its cycles of growth and decline.

In conclusion, Zell and Lurie's method of negotiating business deals merged audacity with carefulness.

They were not afraid to engage in high-risk investments, but they consistently approached them with a thorough awareness of the possible drawbacks and a plan to mitigate those risks.

Their achievement was founded on a careful equilibrium between aspiration and caution, an equilibrium that enabled them to take advantage of chances without stretching themselves too thin.

By utilizing a disciplined method of risk and implementing creative deal-making strategies, Sam Zell and Robert Lurie transformed the real estate sector and created a memorable legacy as expert investors and astute dealmakers.

CHAPTER 6

CHALLENGES AND SETBACKS

6.1 Economic Downturns: Navigating Real Estate Crises

During their remarkable careers, Sam Zell and Robert H. Lurie were recognized not just for their achievements but also for their skill in overcoming major difficulties and economic recessions.

The real estate market is inherently cyclical—flourishing in times of economic growth and shrinking significantly during recessions.

Zell and Lurie, frequently at the forefront of their investments, understood that the capacity to prosper during economic downturns was equally important as achieving success in prosperous times.

Although they established a reputation for identifying opportunities during prosperous periods, it was their reaction to economic downturns that revealed their genuine strength as investors and leaders.

Zell's strategy for economic downturns was based on a philosophy of seizing investment opportunities.

He regarded economic difficulties as inherent parts of the market cycle, instead of as impediments to achievement.

By adopting a mentality of readiness and adaptable strategy, Zell and Lurie effectively reduced their financial risk exposure while taking advantage of the opportunities that came from market declines. One of the defining traits of their partnership was their capacity to stay composed, strategic, and creative in times of crisis.

When the real estate market encountered declines, Zell and Lurie frequently intensified their approach to acquiring undervalued properties.

As numerous investors withdrew during downturns, concerned about additional price declines and market uncertainty, Zell sought chances to purchase troubled properties at a considerable markdown.

By adopting an opposing viewpoint, they successfully created a portfolio of assets at prices significantly lower than market value, setting themselves up for substantial gains when the market finally bounced back. A significant illustration of Zell's talent for taking advantage of a downturn occurred during the recession of the 1990s.

The early 1990s posed significant challenges for real estate investors due to a market characterized by oversupply, increasing interest rates, and a widespread decline in demand.

Instead of withdrawing, Zell and Lurie took advantage of the chance to purchase troubled properties, concentrating on office buildings and retail centers that had lost value due to the economic downturn.

Their profound comprehension of market cycles, combined with their access to funding, enabled them to acquire these assets at reduced prices.

The early 1990s represented a pivotal moment for Zell and Lurie, as they progressed in establishing the basis for what would evolve into their primary real estate portfolio.

While others were hesitant and anticipating economic stability, Zell and Lurie leveraged their skill in recognizing long-term value to expand their business.

They thoughtfully allocated resources to assets that, although affected by the downturn in the short term, possessed considerable promise for value increase as the market started to rebound. Yet, not every decline turned out to be a straightforward obstacle for Zell and Lurie.

The 2008 financial crisis, caused by the collapse of subprime mortgages and the ensuing global recession, posed a significantly tougher challenge.

In contrast to the early 1990s, the 2008 crisis included a widespread collapse of the housing market, a liquidity crunch, and the extensive faltering of financial institutions.

The severity of the crisis complicated Zell and Lurie's ability to locate distressed assets as they had previously done. With the global financial system on the verge of collapse, numerous assets they had gathered were abruptly valued significantly lower than expected.

For Zell, the 2008 financial crisis posed significant difficulties because of his substantial real estate holdings, especially his participation in the Equity Office Properties transaction in 2007.

Zell had sold his publicly traded real estate investment trust (REIT), Equity Office Properties, to Blackstone for $39 billion right before the crisis began.

At first glance, the agreement appeared to be a brilliant move of timing—Zell had effectively left the market right before a downturn. Nonetheless, the wider downturn in international financial markets and its effect on commercial real estate was substantial, and even Zell's keen instincts could not fully shield him from the repercussions of the crisis.

Looking back, although Zell and Lurie's divestment from Equity Office Properties is still lauded, their participation in the commercial real estate sector during the downturn exposed the profound interconnection between the real estate field and the wider economy.

Zell recognized that the crash caught even the most experienced investors off guard, and the repercussions of the crisis were experienced in various sectors.

The financial markets had crumbled, and liquidity was limited, causing even robust players to struggle through the turmoil without facing tough modifications. In reaction to the 2008 crisis, Zell and Lurie modified their approach to prioritize asset preservation.

They optimized processes, divested from low-performing assets, and prioritized sustaining liquidity in their investments. Their capability to adjust to this economic slump was crucial for enduring the aftermath.

Zell's rapid reaction to the shifting economic landscape guaranteed that he and his team stayed financially stable throughout the toughest part of the crisis.

By preserving discipline and remaining dedicated to their long-term investment strategy, Zell and Lurie managed to endure the challenges and eventually emerged more resilient.

Even with their expertise and insight, Zell and Lurie acknowledged the value of gaining knowledge from previous errors.

The 2008 crisis triggered a reevaluation of their risk exposure and resulted in alterations to the way they organized upcoming agreements.

The crisis highlighted the necessity of stress-testing investments and confirming that portfolios had the adaptability to endure economic fluctuations.

Zell and Lurie's capacity to glean insights from their mistakes and enhance their tactics following each challenge became a defining trait of their collaboration, showcasing their toughness when confronted with difficulties.

6.2 Insights Gained: How Challenges Influenced Future Strategy

The difficulties and obstacles that Zell and Lurie encountered throughout their careers were not merely hurdles to surpass; they were insights that influenced their approaches in the future.

Every setback, every crisis, and every close call enabled them to hone their strategy, create new methods, and brace for upcoming unpredictabilities.

Like all successful investors, their lasting success stemmed from their capacity to adapt, learn from experiences, and utilize their errors for future development. A key takeaway from their difficulties was the significance of liquidity.

During the 2008 financial crisis, Zell understood that possessing liquidity—access to cash—was crucial for enduring in a market where credit was scarce and financial entities were hesitant to provide loans.

This experience transformed Zell's investment philosophy in the years that followed.

He grew significantly more conservative with leverage, prioritizing the maintenance of a cash reserve that would enable his companies to withstand market fluctuations. This lesson on liquidity wasn't solely focused on gearing up for economic downturns but also on remaining flexible in the constantly evolving real estate landscape.

Zell also grew more careful about depending on the market's short-term performance.

Although his previous approaches frequently focused on gaining short-term value, like turning over properties for rapid earnings, the repercussions of the 2008 crisis led him to adopt a more long-term perspective on his investments.

He started concentrating on investments with inherent, lasting value—assets that could produce steady cash flow and long-term growth, irrespective of market fluctuations. By concentrating on long-term, stable assets, Zell minimized his vulnerability to abrupt market changes, enhancing his portfolio's strength against potential future declines.

Another insight that Zell and Lurie gained was the importance of diversification. The 2008 crisis underscored the dangers of excessive focus on particular types of real estate or markets.

Although they had consistently taken steps to diversify their portfolio to a degree, the worldwide impact of the 2008 recession emphasized the necessity for greater strategic diversification.

Zell and Lurie broadened their investment scope to encompass global markets and aimed to create portfolios that featured not only commercial real estate but also industrial spaces, residential projects, and additional asset classes such as healthcare and infrastructure.

This diversification assisted in reducing the risks associated with depending too heavily on a single sector and enabled them to take advantage of growth prospects in developing markets.

Alongside diversification, Zell and Lurie understood the significance of flexibility. The real estate market was growing increasingly intricate, as emerging factors such as globalization, technological advancement, and changing demographics impacted demand. Zell and Lurie modified their investment approaches to capitalize on these emerging dynamics.

They adopted technology, utilizing data analytics to enhance investment decisions and grasp market trends more efficiently.

This flexibility not only enabled them to endure economic declines but also set them up for success as the sector transformed.

The insights gained from their failures also transformed their method of negotiating deals. Following the 2008 crisis, Zell adopted a more careful stance toward leverage, choosing to arrange deals that reduced exposure to excessive debt. He also focused more on fostering robust relationships with lenders, partners, and stakeholders, recognizing that trust and cooperation were essential for overcoming challenges.

Zell and Lurie's capability to modify their deal structures and strategies enabled them to navigate the 2008 crisis with little harm to their portfolio.

Ultimately, Zell and Lurie's challenges also enhanced their understanding of the significance of leadership in moments of crisis.

Throughout their careers, they had developed solid teams and reliable advisors, and during economic slumps, the significance of these relationships became increasingly clear. Zell was recognized for his practical leadership approach and his skill in keeping his team engaged and motivated through challenging periods.

His skill in making difficult choices, communicating well with his team, and preserving a sense of hope even in the bleakest times guided his company through some of the toughest economic challenges.

To sum up, the difficulties and obstacles Sam Zell and Robert H. Lurie faced during their careers significantly influenced their methods in real estate and investing.

Every crisis they encountered offered a chance for development, improvement, and adjustment. From their experiences, they discovered that setbacks should not be dreaded but welcomed as chances to learn that could result in even greater achievements.

By staying flexible, broadening their investments, and prioritizing liquidity, Zell and Lurie secured their legacy as two of the most robust and visionary investors in American real estate history.

CHAPTER 7

LEGACY AND LASTING IMPACT

7.1 Shaping the Next Generation: Mentorship and Influence

The legacy of Sam Zell and Robert H. Lurie in real estate goes well beyond the agreements they completed and the firms they created.

Their real influence is in the guidance they offer to future generations of entrepreneurs, investors, and industry leaders.

Through their direction, business strategies, and leadership, Zell and Lurie influenced the real estate sector for many years ahead. Their impact is still evident in the methods and beliefs of numerous leading investors, real estate experts, and business leaders today. Mentorship was a fundamental principle that both Zell and Lurie upheld during their careers.

Their method of mentoring was not the conventional, direct teaching style; rather, it was based on allowing others the liberty to think autonomously, err, and gain insights from their experiences.

They were committed to offering the right chances for driven young individuals and mentoring them in a manner that facilitated development and self-exploration.

This philosophy strongly connected with the teams they formed, fostering a culture of innovation, risk-taking, and resilience.

Zell was especially recognized for his non-intrusive approach to mentoring. He was not the kind of leader who would closely oversee or control the choices made by his team.

Rather, he motivated his team members to take thoughtful risks, adopt an entrepreneurial mindset, and expand their vision. He frequently advised his mentees, "If you aren't failing occasionally, you're not taking enough chances."

Zell's conviction in gaining knowledge from setbacks was a fundamental aspect of his mentorship, and it remains one of the core principles that numerous successful individuals in the real estate sector adhere to today. Zell's guidance reached beyond his own company and permeated the wider business community.

He acted as a reliable consultant for numerous individuals in the real estate and investment fields, leveraging his expertise to offer advice to both novice and experienced business owners.

Zell's talent for identifying potential in others and providing them with important perspectives on market trends, investment tactics, and management approaches enabled him to significantly influence the careers of numerous people.

By inspiring his mentees to adopt unconventional ideas and chase ambitious objectives, Zell established a lasting ripple effect that keeps shaping the future of real estate professionals.

Robert Lurie, though similarly impactful in molding the real estate scene, adopted a somewhat distinct perspective on mentorship.

Recognized for his analytical precision and emphasis on operational superiority, Lurie's guidance concentrated significantly on enhancing the technical and financial skills of his mentees.

Lurie excelled in deal structuring and was enthusiastic about sharing his expertise in financial models, due diligence, and market analysis with others. His focus on grasping the intricacies of the real estate sector provided young professionals with the resources essential for thriving in a frequently unpredictable field.

Lurie also focused heavily on establishing strong, enduring relationships. He thought that achieving success in real estate involved not only the deals you closed but also the individuals you collaborated with.

For Lurie, mentoring involved showing others ways to establish trust and credibility in the field.

He often urged young professionals to "regard your business connections as family," recognizing that respect and integrity would yield lasting benefits.

Both Zell and Lurie played a key role in promoting a culture of teamwork within their organizations.

They recognized the value of collaboration and frequently discussed how their partnership exemplified a blueprint for those they guided.

Zell and Lurie were not just business partners; they were also close friends who encouraged and tested one another.

This dynamic enhanced their mentorship significantly, as they frequently offered various viewpoints to those they mentored.

While Zell promoted taking risks and decisive actions, Lurie focused on careful planning and strategic implementation.

Their collaborative method offered a thorough educational experience for individuals who engaged with them.

Zell and Lurie actively sought and developed talent from various backgrounds, making certain that the real estate sector continued to be an inclusive and vibrant industry.

Both individuals supported the advancement of varied voices in positions of leadership.

Their businesses were recognized for promoting an atmosphere where women and minorities could succeed, contributing to a more varied and inventive workforce within the real estate sector.

By promoting diversity, Zell and Lurie not only strengthened their businesses but also established a standard for future leadership in the industry.

The impact of Zell and Lurie is evident in the careers of numerous accomplished individuals within the real estate sector.

Their mentee, Tony James, who later became the president of Blackstone, acknowledges Zell for teaching him the significance of "prioritizing relationships over deals."

James' professional journey embodies the overarching mentorship framework established by Zell and Lurie, where achievements were frequently gauged by the quality of connections rather than just financial outcomes. Their influence also reached their organizations. Both individuals played a key role in developing a new wave of leaders in their organizations, many of whom later emerged as significant personalities in the real estate sector.

Zell's company, Equity Group Investments, along with Lurie's enterprises like Lurie Investments, turned into hubs for developing talent.

The culture established in their companies centered around innovation, risk management, and relationship-building, emerged as a blueprint for the entire real estate industry.

Although Zell and Lurie gained recognition for their achievements, their talent for mentoring and motivating the upcoming generation of business leaders may be their most lasting legacy.

With their guidance, they conveyed not only the techniques of real estate investment but also the attitude required to thrive in a constantly changing and competitive field.

Their impact continues to be significant, influencing the choices of contemporary leaders in real estate and other fields.

7.2 Lasting Effects: The Ongoing Impact of Zell & Lurie on Real Estate

The enduring impact of Sam Zell and Robert Lurie on the real estate sector is indisputable.

Through the years, their creative methods in investing, transaction-making, and business oversight have established the benchmark for excellence in the industry.

The combined influence of Zell and Lurie has transcended the modification of specific companies; it has revolutionized the overall real estate environment, bringing forth innovative strategies, frameworks, and models that still influence the sector today.

A key element of Zell and Lurie's lasting influence is their contribution to the development and promotion of Real Estate Investment Trusts (REITs).

In the early 1990s, Zell and Lurie identified the opportunity for REITs to transform the processes of buying, selling, and managing real estate.

They realized that by providing a liquid means for investing in real estate assets, REITs could engage a broader spectrum of investors, especially institutional ones, and make high-quality real estate portfolios more accessible.

The emergence of REITs transformed the real estate market by allowing smaller investors to access large commercial properties and developments without the necessity of purchasing or managing the properties independently. Zell's Equity Residential, among the largest REITs globally, set a standard for the sector, and its achievements showcased the worth of REITs as an investment category.

The model they developed enabled investors to combine their funds and invest in properties that would likely have been inaccessible, thereby fostering considerable expansion in the real estate market.

Zell and Lurie's influence on the real estate sector also included their knack for recognizing and taking advantage of new markets and trends. They were pioneers in the concept that real estate investment could be an international endeavor, unrestricted by geographical limits.

With the rise of globalization in the late 20th and early 21st centuries, Zell and Lurie were pioneers in investigating international real estate markets, understanding the chance to diversify portfolios and grow their businesses internationally.

Their worldwide strategy contributed to transforming the real estate sector into the multinational, interconnected domain it has become today.

Alongside their emphasis on worldwide growth, Zell and Lurie acknowledged the significance of technological advancement in the real estate sector. Although numerous individuals in the industry were hesitant to embrace new technologies, Zell and Lurie were early advocates for leveraging technology to enhance operational efficiency, optimize management practices, and assess market trends.

Zell, specifically, gained recognition for his adoption of data analysis and technology-based investment approaches. His conviction that technology serves as a means for improved decision-making was a key factor in his success.

Zell's impact also reached beyond the field of real estate investment. He emerged as a reliable voice within the wider business community, often addressing topics concerning business strategy, economic policy, and leadership.

Zell's philosophical perspective on risk and innovation established him as a highly regarded speaker and advisor, with his opinions on entrepreneurship and investing earning widespread respect.

His position as a thought leader in the business community contributed to raising the profile of real estate as a career and drawing in new talent to the industry.

In addition to their financial achievements, Zell and Lurie's dedication to social responsibility and corporate governance left a lasting impression. Both individuals valued the significance of ethical business practices and social responsibility, understanding that enduring success in real estate could not rely solely on profits but also on the quality of the connections they developed with communities, stakeholders, and employees.

This ideology was clear in their strategy for acquisitions and investments, as they aimed to generate value not only for themselves but also for the wider community.

In summary, the enduring influence of Sam Zell and Robert Lurie on the real estate sector is significant and complex. By pioneering the creation of REITs, adopting technology, growing internationally, and promoting a culture of mentorship, they have made a lasting impact on the industry.

Their creative approaches and guidance have motivated generations of investors, executives, and entrepreneurs to dream larger, embrace calculated risks, and prioritize long-term value generation.

Zell and Lurie's impact will persist in influencing the future of real estate for many years, securing their status as two of the most significant individuals in the history of American real estate.